I Love Sports

Softball

by Cari Meister

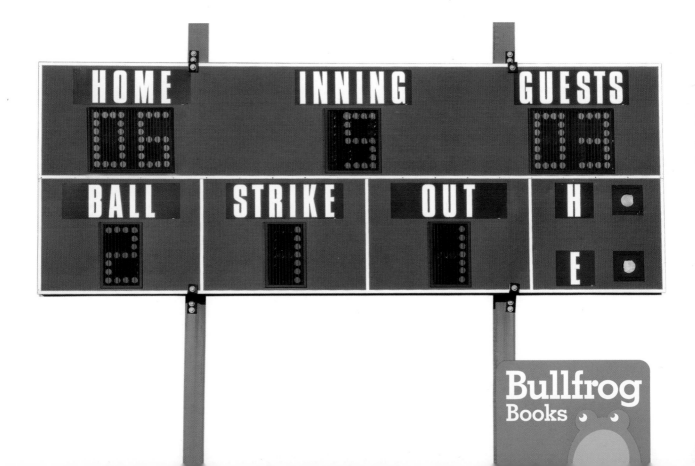

Bullfrog Books

Ideas for Parents and Teachers

Bullfrog Books let children practice reading informational text at the earliest reading levels. Repetition, familiar words, and photo labels support early readers.

Before Reading

- Discuss the cover photo. What does it tell them?

- Look at the picture glossary together. Read and discuss the words.

Read the Book

- "Walk" through the book and look at the photos. Let the child ask questions. Point out the photo labels.

- Read the book to the child, or have him or her read independently.

After Reading

- Prompt the child to think more. Ask: Have you ever played softball? What position did you play?

Bullfrog Books are published by Jump!
5357 Penn Avenue South
Minneapolis, MN 55419
www.jumplibrary.com

Library of Congress Cataloging-in-Publication Data

Names: Meister, Cari, author.
Title: Softball / by Cari Meister.
Description: Minneapolis, MN: Jump!, Inc. [2017]
Series: I love sports | Includes index.
Identifiers: LCCN 2016007139 (print)
LCCN 2016007792 (ebook)
ISBN 9781620313626 (hardcover: alk. paper)
ISBN 9781624964091 (ebook)
Subjects: LCSH: Softball—Juvenile literature.
Classification: LCC GV881.M45 2017 (print)
LCC GV881 (ebook) | DDC 796.357/8—dc23
LC record available at http://lccn.loc.gov/2016007139

Editor: Jenny Fretland VanVoorst
Series Designer: Ellen Huber
Book Designer: Molly Ballanger
Photo Researcher: Molly Ballanger

Photo Credits: All photos by Shutterstock except: Chad McDermott/Shutterstock.com, 6–7; iStock, 4, 23bl; Thinkstock, 5, 14–15, 16–17, 20–21, 23ml, 23tr; 123RF, cover.

Printed in the United States of America at Corporate Graphics in North Mankato, Minnesota.

Table of Contents

Let's Play Softball!

Put on a helmet.
Grab a bat.

Let's play softball!

Anna is first at bat.

Ruby pitches.

Anna swings.

Crack!

She hits the ball.

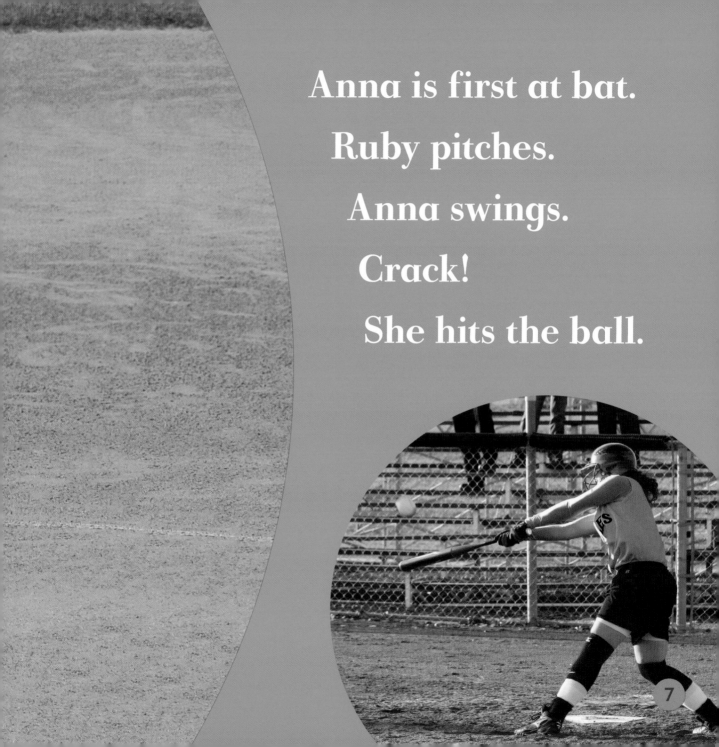

Anna runs to first base.

She is safe.

base

Now it is Jed's turn.

He swings.

He misses.

"Strike one," yells the ump.

Ruby pitches.
Jed swings.
He hits the ball.

May catches
it in her glove.

Jed is out.

After three outs,
the teams switch.

Batter up!

Rex hits the ball.

It goes far.

It is a home run!

Rex runs around the bases.

He scores a run.

**The team with
the most runs wins.**

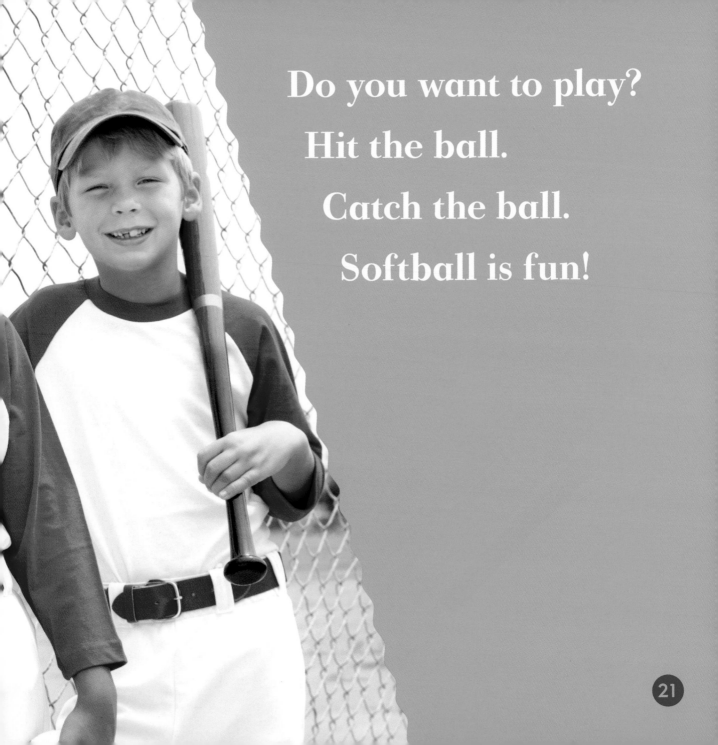

Do you want to play?
Hit the ball.
Catch the ball.
Softball is fun!

21

At the Softball Field

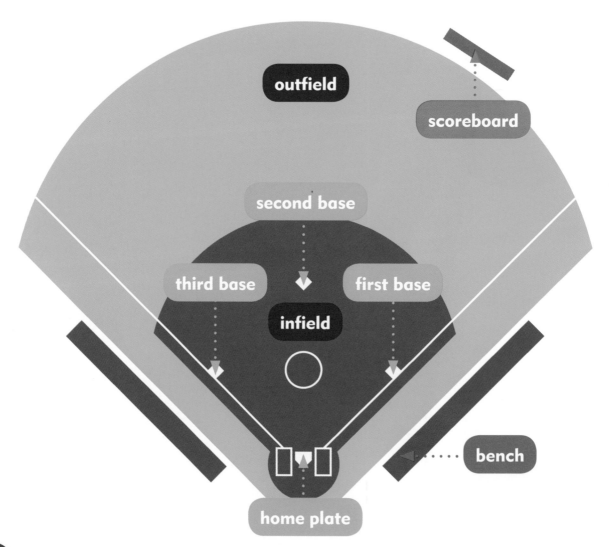

Picture Glossary

base
A station
a runner
in softball
must touch in
order to score.

home run
When a batter
hits the ball and
runs around all
the bases without
getting out.

glove
A large leather
covering for
the hand used
for catching
softballs.

pitch
To throw a softball
for the batter to
try to hit; softball
pitchers throw the
ball underhand.

helmet
A hard hat used
to protect a
player's head.

ump
The person
in charge of
making sure
the teams
follow the rules.

Index

To Learn More

Learning more is as easy as 1, 2, 3.

1) Go to www.factsurfer.com

2) Enter "softball" into the search box.

3) Click the "Surf" button to see a list of websites.

With factsurfer.com, finding more information is just a click away.

15·80